A SPIRIT DAUGHTER WORKBOOK

WRITTEN BY
JILL WINTERSTEEN

FOR THE FULL MOON

WEDNESDAY, OCTOBER 20TH, 2021
7:56 AM PT

THE FULL MOON

Every Sun Season has its Full Moon positioned in the opposite zodiac sign. While the Sun sits in Libra, the Moon lands in Aries, giving us our Full Moon. The energy created by the Sun and Moon facing each other encourages us to pause, reflect, and release what we no longer want to carry. The Full Moon slows us down, both by her beauty and her vibration. On the New Moon, we plant intentions and envision our evolution. The Full Moon asks us how those visions are unfolding. During this period of reflection, the Moon reveals where we may be blocking our intentions from manifesting. It shows us the work we must do within ourselves to create the life of our highest visions. The Full Moon illuminates our shadows and gives us guidance on how to shift them into the light.

Every zodiac energy has a high side and a low side. On a Full Moon, the Sun and the Moon signs form an axis of energy for us to work with in our energetic bodies. The Full Moon helps us understand the higher and lower frequencies of the signs involved. We can then become aware of how we align with these frequencies in our thoughts, emotions, and behaviors. Our current Full Moon brings us the vibrations of Aries and Libra. No matter our personal signs, we all align with aspects of these energies at different points in our lives. The Full Moon shows us how we embody the frequencies of the two zodiac signs involved and how we can raise our vibration through them.

As we release and shift the vibrations that resonate us away from who we want to be, we unblock ourselves. We free our energy to take on the higher frequencies of the Sun and Moon signs. The Full Moon shows us how we can direct the astrological signs' positive aspects into manifesting the visions planted on the New Moon. It takes work to shift and release frequencies we no longer want in our lives. Many of these energies have been with us for some time and may not want to let go. The Full Moon is about building awareness of the work we need to do while understanding that this work may not occur overnight. Shifts can happen quickly, but they also can take continual awareness on our part to ensure the change we want to see becomes permanent.

Shifting our vibration can occur with a single change in perception or a new understanding. Our energy can work like a light switch, where one moment we are vibrating at a certain level, then the next we exist at a whole new level. Finding the light switch, though, can be the challenging part. Shifting patterns in our emotions or releasing long-held beliefs requires finding the root cause of what we are trying to change. It requires awareness and deep understanding. Going into the shadows of ourselves can be frightening, but with the Full Moon's help, we can go into the places we usually hide to find the switch that will help us change everything.

As we do the work of each Full Moon, we provide ourselves a blueprint for our evolution. Each month, we gain a new set of energies to understand, unravel, and transform. These vibrations correspond to the astrological signs of the Sun and Moon. As we make our way through all twelve Full Moons in a year, we touch on every aspect of ourselves. We open the door for transformation and affirmation of the aspects we want to nourish. Full Moons help us release, but they also help us embrace the vibrations we want to carry. They help us recognize our strengths, our power, and our light. As we work with each Full Moon, we can step away from each sign's lower frequencies and into the higher ones. There is an opportunity to see ourselves in full view, including the traits we want to support and show to the world.

ARIES FULL MOON

TUNE INTO YOUR INTERNAL FIRE

Near the end of Libra Season, we are greeted by the Aries Full Moon asking us to focus on ourselves, our purpose, and our soul's journey. Aries is the warrior of the zodiac. This energy encourages us to take action, fight for what we believe in, and overcome any obstacles in the way of our dreams. This Full Moon always proves to be an exciting one and an opportunity to feel our life's mission, then decide how to pursue it. Over this Full Moon, give yourself space away from the partnerships you've been working on for the last four weeks and focus on you. What do you want? What does your soul want?

ARIES FULL MOON

Ruled by fire and the planet Mars, Aries teaches us that we are each here on a mission. Our soul wants to accomplish something this lifetime. Each of us has a purpose, and it will keep calling us until we pay attention to it. It may take years for us to find our purpose, then even longer to follow it. Knowing your mission in life is not an easy feat. Some people will know it their whole lives, while others will travel the world trying to find it. You do not need to know your life's purpose right now. This Full Moon can help you feel it, though, if you allow it. Once you know your purpose, it's then up to you to pursue it.

Pursuing your purpose in life can feel daunting. It may require career shifts or big moves to new locations. It may also ask you to say goodbye to certain people or habits. This Full Moon helps us recognize anything that is in the way of us pursuing our purpose, then release it. Aries brings us courage and motivation. Feel these vibrations this Full Moon to let go of habits, projects, and other energies that block you from aligning with the life your soul wants to live. Feel the warrior spirit of Aries and decide what you are willing to fight for in your life. What battle is worth your energy?

This Full Moon is also a time to look at how you may be battling with yourself. Are you fighting your soul's calling? Or ignoring it? Notice if you are instilling doubts in yourself that block you from pursuing your life's mission. Each astrological energy has a low side and high side. For Aries, the lower frequency is frustration and anger. When we don't follow our soul's purpose, we tend to end up frustrated with life and angry at ourselves. We may also become angry at the people around us as we project our frustrations onto them. This Full Moon is a time to feel any anger you may have and find its origin. Are you frustrated that you are not living the life of your soul? Have you made compromises on things that needed to be fought for instead?

Notice if you waged war on yourself. With the help of this Full Moon, transform your anger into motivation. Aries can help you tune into your internal fire. You can direct that fire either at yourself or into making changes that help you align with your soul. Instead of attacking yourself with limiting beliefs or self-sabotaging messages, take bold steps on your personal journey. Use your fire to take action in creating the life you want to live. Stop ignoring the callings of your soul and instead listen, then follow them. Create a life that makes you feel content on all levels and leaves no room for anger over what could have been.

This Full Moon can also help us reignite our passion if we have lost it. Once we find our purpose and pursue it, it can become challenging to stay motivated. We may end up feeling stagnant in our growth, or like we are trapped by our mission. Keeping up your passion for life is an important part of following your soul's journey. During this Full Moon, feel into any resentment you may have for your purpose. Does it make you feel trapped? How can you shift the way you feel about it? Trying seeing your life's mission as an opportunity to evolve and accomplish something your soul may have been trying to fulfill for many lifetimes. Fall in love with your mission again and again by recognizing that it's the reason you are here this lifetime. You and only you can pursue your life's journey. It is a special voyage designed for you by you. Be grateful for your path and how you found it. Be grateful for the people who have helped and supported you. And be grateful for being you.

ARIES MOON X LIBRA SUN

While the Moon lands in Aries, the Sun remains in Libra, allowing us to work with both of these vibrations in our energetic bodies. On Full Moons, the Sun opposes the Moon, revealing a spectrum of energies, both high and low. We have the opportunity to release any lower frequencies we may be aligning with and transform them into higher ones. It starts, though, by being aware of what frequencies are available to us to work on during a Full Moon, then becoming aware of which ones we are aligning with in our behaviors, thoughts, and emotions.

Aries and Libra sit opposite each other in the sky and on the zodiac wheel. Aries is home to the First House of the self and ruled by Mars, while Libra is home to the Seventh House of relationships and ruled by Venus. On the surface, these two energies are as different as can be. When we look a little closer, they can teach us valuable lessons about staying aligned with our soul's journey while sharing the experience of living it with another.

Aries reminds us this Full Moon that we have a purpose in this life, and when we find it, we feel content. Libra encourages us to feel at peace no matter the situation, which is more easily achieved when aligned with our soul's path. Furthermore, we have a better chance of forming healthy relationships and partnerships when we have a purpose and feel fulfilled on our own. This Full Moon reminds us that we are already whole. People in our lives do not complete us. Instead, they make life that much sweeter. The real relationship to observe during this season is the one with yourself.

Aries and Libra both carry the warrior spirit. Aries is more aggressive, depicting the typical warrior ready to fight through adversity to rise to the next level. Libra is more of a peaceful warrior, who battles only when balance has been disturbed. Aries gives us the energy to conquer some of our toughest demons, while Libra helps us right the wrongs done to us or those we've done to others. Aries also fights with fire and force, while Libra uses air composed of words and balanced communications. Aries, though, is direct and often unstoppable. When we invoke the energy of Aries, change happens. We send the message, and there is no misinterpreting the meaning. Libra, on the other hand, is softer and often can be swayed to another side. Libra tends to see all sides equally, which can be beneficial. But it can also make this energy less effective in creating change quickly. The vibration of Libra asks that we first understand the whole issue from all sides before making a decision. This understanding can take time and may lose momentum.

When we look at Aries's higher vibrations, we see courage, determination, stamina and drive. This energy helps us make decisions quickly and confidently. It also helps us dissolve obstacles with determination and sheer willpower. This is the energy of the Ram, ready to act when needed and not allowing anything to stop it. We need this energy in our lives when we are facing adversities, starting something new, or choosing to focus on ourselves. It allows us to make challenging choices that demand we put ourselves first. It also helps us understand when being selfish can be beneficial for our evolution and the overall vibration of the world. Aries teaches us that when we put ourselves and our missions first, everyone benefits. Our path may require us to choose it over and over again. Aries gives us the energy needed to choose our soul's journey even when it's not the easy one.

Aries in its low, or shadow, frequencies does become negatively selfish. When we align with this side, we forget that we live in a world full of other people. We lose our ability to compromise or make choices for the sake of peace. We stand our ground even when it's not worth the battle. We may even start battles just for the sake of proving a point with no real intention behind the energy. Aries's lower frequencies cause us to make ourselves the only priority. It also causes us to focus on only our perspective, giving us a one-sided vision, as we forget to see things from another's point of view.

ARIES MOON X LIBRA SUN

Selfishness is a fine line. We need enough of it to stay true to our journey and not give into other people's demands when they challenge our commitment to ourselves. Too much selfishness, though, causes us to live a life of solitude or unbalanced relationships. When we take too much energy, it doesn't feel good. We intuitively know when relationships are unbalanced. We may not know how to correct it, but we know that something if off. This feeling of imbalance causes frustration and anger—other low sides of Aries. As you work with the Full Moon, ask yourself where you may have crossed the line of selfishness. Where do you need to be more selfish for the sake of your soul? And where do you need to be less selfish for the sake of your partnerships? Align with the Full Moon to shift these energies. Make yourself a priority, but also know where and how you can compromise. There are things in this life that are non-negotiable, and there are things that we can loosen our grip on. Decide on this Full Moon what you are willing to fight for, what you are willing to stand your ground on, and what you are willing to negotiate over for another person's happiness. Helping others be happy in turn makes us happy in our hearts and can sometimes be more important than proving a point.

This Full Moon also helps us shed the lower vibrations of Libra, which can work against the search for our purpose. The low, or shadow, side of the scales is passive-aggressiveness and indecision. When we align with this side, we vacillate between choices and often become frustrated. We cannot decide on a path, and we question our instinctual knowledge. We lose trust in ourselves and can run around in circles, never finding our way. Being indecisive is another way we battle with ourselves, and this war can spill onto others. This constant wavering can pressure our relationships as we look to others for answers, not understanding that we already hold the answers we seek. We also tend to lean on others' support instead of our own inner strength to help us on our journeys. This behavior can lead to codependency and a sense of losing ourselves in another.

If you find yourself aligning with the lower vibrations of Libra, it's best to spend some time in meditation, learning to trust yourself without outside influence. Ask yourself some questions and notice the first answers that appear. Do not overanalyze them, but allow them to come from your intuition. Feel your gut response and go with it. Take action and know that if things don't go the way you want them to, there will always be a lesson to learn and room to grow. Give yourself the grace to make missteps on your path. This allowance will encourage you to pick a road and walk it.

As we step away from the lower vibrations of Aries and Libra, we allow ourselves to align with our soul's purpose. We understand that when we feel content and fulfilled, everyone in our life benefits. We can balance the priority and responsibility to ourselves with our responsibilities to others. We know when to compromise, when to fight for what we love, and how to make peace with our soul's journey. This Full Moon has the power to teach us about our soul's purpose and how to pursue it while living in the world with other people—each of whom has their own soul's purpose. When we integrate the higher vibrations of Libra and Aries, we know how to support both ourselves and others. We also know when to ask for support and even choose partners who help evolve us to the next level of our personal journey.

This Moon can help you understand your journey more deeply and in turn help you develop more fulfilling relationships. Ideally, you want partners who also understand how to balance their life's mission with yours so that each person feels fulfilled and without resentment. Align with this Full Moon to create a life full of purpose, passion, and enjoyment. Then learn how to make it a priority while still sharing the experience and joy of life with others.

08

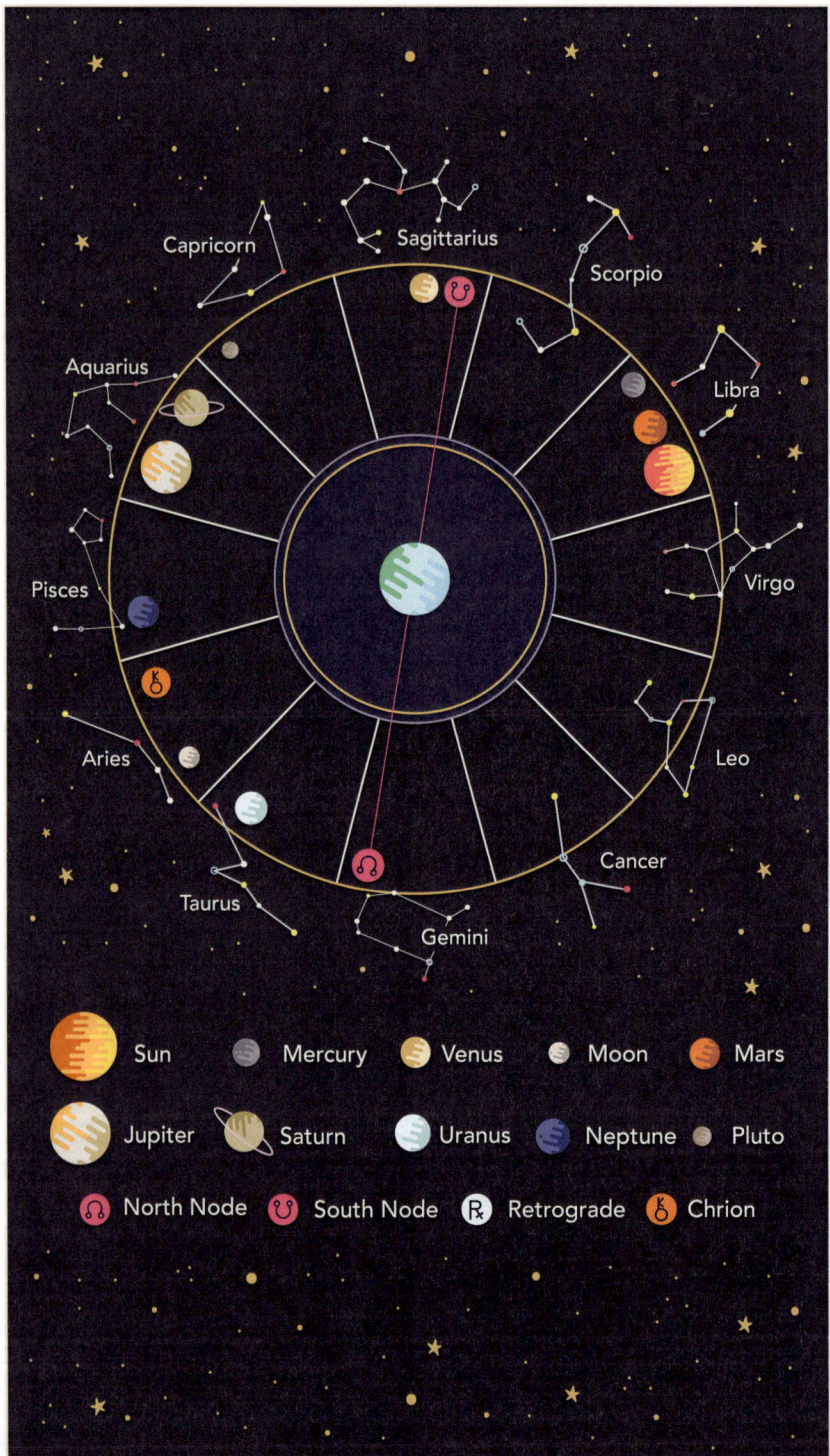

ASPECTS

The Moon and Sun do not exist in the sky alone. There are other planets, each with its own energies, that affect the Full Moon. The planets we are most concerned with on a Full Moon create aspects with the Sun and Moon. An aspect is a degree of separation. When cosmic bodies are specific degrees away from each other, they create vibrations that we feel along with the energies of the Full Moon. The main aspect of any Full Moon is the 180-degree separation of the Moon and Sun. This opposition causes tension as it reveals layers of energy that are often hidden or buried in the subconscious. This tension, though, is what creates breakthroughs in our consciousness and allows us to grow, evolve, and transform.

In addition to the opposition formed by the Sun and Moon, this Full Moon has a few other aspects to work with energetically. The Sun in conjunct, or right next to, Mars in Libra. Aries, on the other side of the sky, opposes Mars. Mars is the planetary ruler of Aries, so these aspects make for an interesting addition to our Full Moon's energy. Mars in Libra is somewhat out of place. Mars is full of fire and compels us to take quick action. Libra, on the other hand, strives for peace and is much more subdued in its energy compared to Mars. Mars doesn't quite know what to do in Libra. Its placement there encourages us to make decisions regarding our relationships. It may even cause us to act without thinking first. It's important to resist the urge to rush into or out of any commitments when Mars is in Libra. Align with Libra to breathe deeply and approach your relationships from a place of calmness instead of fire.

With Mars in Libra opposing the Full Moon, we need to be especially aware of making harsh or quick reactions to our partners. Mars is challenging us this Full Moon, and the best way to work with this energy is to be acutely aware of how we feel. If you find yourself experiencing intense emotions at any point, spend some time trying to understand them before acting on them. For instance, if you feel a sudden rush of anger, try sitting with it and asking it where it came from. Often when we feel anger it's because our boundaries have been crossed on some level. Try to understand the origin of the feeling before speaking about it with another. It can also be helpful to move your body and energy when the Moon is in Aries. Go for a run or break a sweat in some other way to help create a free flow of energy through your body. When energy stagnates, it can cause frustration and other negative emotions, all of which will be intensified by the Aries Full Moon.

We also have an aspect with Pluto to work with this Full Moon. Pluto helps you process trauma and pain. It teaches you to understand that your life is a small fraction of the many life cycles your soul has experienced. Pluto helps us place past events against the framework of the larger picture of our many lives. It also helps us heal from our pain through acknowledging that vastness of our soul and the evolution it is on.

The Sun and Moon form square, a 90° aspect, with Pluto this Full Moon. Square aspects can create a feeling of friction in our lives. With the intense energy of Aries, this aspect may cause us to feel angry or resentful about past circumstances. We may even find ourselves thinking about or feeling emotions from the past. If painful memories seem to be surfacing for you, look for the opportunity to heal them this Full Moon. Ask yourself if there is someone you need to forgive. You may even need to forgive yourself. Forgiveness is a form a letting go and can be one of the hardest forms of release. Once we forgive, though, we release past pain, anger, and regret. We can heal and move forward in life. As Aries inspires you to take steps on your journey this Full Moon, feel if the past is blocking your growth and decision-making. Align with the Full Moon to heal from your past and loosen yourself from its grip, allowing yourself to move freely toward your soul's purpose.

HOUSESCOPES

While the Full Moon in Aries will affect us all, we can look more specifically at where we will feel this energy most intensely through understanding our houses. Astrological houses represent areas of our lives. We each have twelve houses in our natal charts, one of which is governed by Aries. This house tells us which area of life will feel the effects of this Full Moon. Below is a guide on how to work with this Full Moon depending on which house is ruled by Aries in your chart. You can look up your chart at astro-charts.com.

Aries First House: The First House informs your decisions and how you move forward in life. It is the part of yourself that you project outwardly and is often people's first impression of you. With Aries here, you are full of energy and fire. Everyone can see your passion for life, and you are quick to start any projects, both with others and alone. On the Full Moon, feel how you can keep your fire burning even when the initial excitement wears off. Let go of the notion that life has to be exciting to be wonderful. Sometimes the most precious moments occur in the calmest seas.

Aries Second House: The Second House governs how you experience resources. It helps form your expectations of finances and how you manifest abundance in your life. With Aries here, you may be impulsive when it comes to spending or making money. You may also not have a lot of patience when it comes to waiting for abundance to find you. Aries compels you to make things happen, but sometimes the best thing you can do is assume it's already happening. On the Full Moon, work on sitting still and feeling your inherent worth. Attract what you need through your vibration instead of forcing things to occur.

Aries Third House: The Third House governs how you communicate and exchange ideas. It shows the languages you use, both overtly and subtly. It also governs how you receive information and listen. With Aries here, you are bold in your communication. You exchange information rather dramatically and with your full spirit behind it. You are a passionate speaker and are able to inspire a crowd. On the Full Moon, experiment with different styles of speaking and different ways of communicating. Not everyone can receive your boisterous vibrations; try lowering the volume to where you be really understood, seen, and heard by the people in your life.

Aries Fourth House: The Fourth House governs your home, both internal and external. It guides you in making choices about who you live with and where you live. It also helps you choose who becomes your soul family and inner circle. With Aries here, you may be quick to move from one location to another. You may also shy away from deeper connections with others. On the Full Moon, recognize your need for change and, in this awareness, give yourself the space to stay sill. Open up to others and let them into your world. Remember that love is what happens when you stay.

Aries Fifth House: The Fifth House governs how you create, express yourself, and enjoy life. It determines how you play and connect with your inner child. With Aries here, you have a lust for life. You enjoy every moment of it, but you may take it a bit too seriously. Remember to take vacations and slow your speed for a moment. When you slow down, you move more quickly when you start again. On the Full Moon, find ways to turn your fire into creativity. Express yourself in a new way that honors your inner child and gives you space to connect more deeply with the elements of life.

Aries Sixth House: The Sixth House governs how you show up for others. It directs you in making choices that serve others. It also guides you in making selfless decisions. With Aries here, your challenge is to find how your personal journey also helps others. This placement asks you to recognize that when you align with your soul, you help raise the vibration of the world. On the Full Moon, reconcile any blocks you have against serving or helping humanity. Release any resistance of resentment and accept that this is part of your path and will always be, no matter what you do. Your life's mission involves helping humanity in some way.

Aries Seventh House: The Seventh House governs partnerships and how you connect with others. It informs how you choose relationships and show up in those relationships. With Aries here, you may find it challenging to see another person's point of view. With some awareness, though, you can really step into another person's shoes and help prioritize your needs and the needs of the other person. On this Full Moon, remember to ask for what you need before you become angry about it. Find ways to say what you need to say through calmness and peace.

Aries Eighth House: The Eighth House governs your personal growth and the lessons you will endure this lifetime for the sake of evolution. With Aries here, you seek experiences that excite and challenge you. You grow through adversity and often attract stressful situations in order to evolve. You can handle it all, though, with courage and the inner knowing that you can overcome anything. On the Full Moon, feel into what is showing up for you in the realm of personal growth. Release any fear that you are not ready and take the plunge into a new reality that brings change and growth, and aligns you with your soul.

Aries Ninth House: The Ninth House governs how you find, integrate, and attract new knowledge. It is also the house of travel, but this travel is for the sake of expansion. With Aries here, you are quick to assimilate new ideas and experiences. You seek out novel experiences that challenge you and ask you to grow. On the Full Moon, let yourself wander. Go somewhere you haven't been before or visit with people you haven't seen in a while. Introduce yourself to new knowledge and maybe even cultures, and allow yourself to grow through them.

Aries Tenth House: The Tenth House governs your career and how you integrate it with your life's mission. This house affects how you show up in the world and what you allow others to see. It, in essence, is your reputation and represents how you want to be seen. With Aries here, you want your life's mission known to the world. You desire to be seen as strong, willful, and motivated. You take you career seriously, although you may change jobs frequently until you find the right fit. On the Full Moon, let go of any doubt that you can't have it all, because you can. Align with the Full Moon to feel what your true purpose is, then make it the center of your life.

Aries Eleventh House: The Eleventh House governs your friends and community. It guides you in acting within the collective and determines how you show up for the people you know. With Aries here, you are a natural leader. You have a bright spirit that inspires everyone. You may initially resist being a leader, but you eventually will see that it serves everyone if you step into this role. On the Full Moon, consider how your life's mission affects the collective. Release any doubts or fears about your brilliance and show up as the powerful leader you are.

Aries Twelfth House: The Twelfth House governs your spiritual growth. It guides you in making choices around spirituality, including the rituals and practices you choose to make a center of your life. With Aries here, you may find it difficult to slow down long enough to dive deep into practices like meditation or yoga. These practices, though, are the key that unlocks your passions and strong willpower. On the Full Moon, challenge yourself to go on a spiritual quest. Spend time alone with yourself and without distractions. Sit in meditation, take a walk in nature, or journal some of the harder questions you are facing. Feel your potential to be one with your spiritual nature this Full Moon.

ARIES LUNAR FLOW

Sun Salutation A // 3 Rounds

Stand at the top of your mat. Inhale, stretch your arms overhead > Exhale, fold forward > Inhale, lengthen out your back > Exhale, step back to Plank Pose and lower > Inhale, reach your chest up for Cobra Pose, legs on the ground > Exhale, Downward Dog Pose. Stay here for 5 breaths and feel your entire body expand. On exhale, step to the top of your mat > Inhale, lengthen through your spine > Exhale, fold forward > Inhale, come all the way up to standing, reaching arms overhead > Exhale, hands to your heart. Pause for a moment and feel yourself centered throughout your body.

Sun Salutation B // 3 Rounds

Stand at the top of your mat. Inhale, stretch your arms overhead, and bend your knees into Chair Pose > Exhale, fold forward > Inhale, lengthen out your back > Exhale, step into Plank Pose and lower half way to Chatarunga (elbows into ribs) > Inhale, reach your chest up for Upward-Facing Dog, with everything off the ground except your hands and feet > Exhale, Downward Dog Pose > Inhale, step left foot forward to Warrior 1, with your back foot flat at a 45-degree angle. Bend into your front knee and lift your arms to the sky, taking 5 breaths here > Exhale, release into Plank > lower to Chatarunga > Inhale into Upward-Facing Dog > Exhale, Downward Facing Dog. Repeat on right side, then remain in Downward Dog for 5 breaths > Exhale, step to the top of your mat > Inhale, lengthen through your spine > Exhale, fold forward > Inhale, Chair Pose > Exhale, hands to heart, breathe at the top of your mat as you feel your energy circulating throughout your body.

Warrior 2 > Extended Warrior > Triangle Pose

Step your feet three to four feet wide on your mat facing the side. Turn your left foot toward the back of the mat and angle your back foot to 45 degrees. Bend in your front knee and reach your arms out to either side. Breathe here for 5 breaths and feel your hips open. After 5 breaths, place your left forearm to your left thigh and extend your right arm in line with your ear. Take 5 more breaths here. Begin to feel the strength of your legs supporting you, reminding you of your warrior spirit. During inhale, come back up to Warrior 2, straighten your front leg, and hinge forward into Triangle Pose. Place your left hand on the ground on the outside of your left foot or on your shin, and rotate your torso to the right. Stretch and reach

upward through your right arm, feeling one long line of energy from fingertip to fingertip. After 5 breaths, come back upright and return your feet to parallel. Feel the strength of your body, which is ready to take on any challenge. Repeat on your right side.

Standing Apanasana > Warrior 3 > Lunge Pose

Step back to the top of your mat. Feel both feet on the ground as you steady your gaze. Shift your weight into your left foot. Pick your right foot off the ground, bending your knee and hugging it into the chest for standing Apanasana. Take 5 breaths here as you reach up through your chest and press down through your left foot. Without placing your foot down, release your knee and stretch your right leg back behind you, tilting your torso forward parallel to the ground for Warrior 3. You may press your hands together at heart center or reach your arms forward for the full pose. Take 5 breaths here, then place your left foot on the ground behind you for Lunge Pose. Tilt your pelvis down to the ground and stretch your arms up to the sky. Press firmly though your back leg as you bend to a 90-degree angle in your front leg. Take 5 breaths here, then step back to the top of your mat and repeat on the other side.

Side Plank

From the top of your mat, inhale as you reach your arms overhead. Exhale, fold forward. Inhale, lengthen out your back. Exhale, step back into a Plank Pose. Hold as you shift your weight to your left hand. Pivot both feet to the left, stacking your right foot over your left (toes pointing to the right side of your mat). Rotate your chest to the right as you reach your right arm to the ceiling. Draw your lower belly in, directing your tailbone to your heels. Expand through your chest as you draw your shoulders down your back. Take 5 breaths here, feeling the heat and strength building in your core. After 5 breaths, come back to Plank Pose. Rest if you need to, then switch sides. Afterward, press back into Downward Dog and take 5 deep breaths. On exhale, step your feet to the top of your mat. Inhale, lengthen out your back. Exhale, fold forward. Inhale, come up to standing while reaching your arms overhead. Exhale, hands to heart center.

Squat Pose with Breath of Fire

Separate your feet hips width apart, and turn your toes out to 45 degrees. Sit down into a squat; if needed, place a rolled-up towel underneath your heels. Bring your hands to your heart and press your elbows into your legs, opening your hips. Lengthen through your spine and take a deep inhale. During exhale, make short, sharp exhales through your nose, snapping your belly back to your spine. Pump your belly for 20 rounds, focusing only on the exhale. Once completed, take another deep inhale and hold the breath for 10 seconds, then exhale completely.

Savasana

Release onto the floor, lying with your palms up and eyes closed. Feel your body alive with fresh energy circulating freely through your body.

FULL MOON MEDITATION

Breath of Fire is a rhythmic breath focused on the exhale. It helps move the energy of the body, breaking up any stagnation. It also helps create motivation by fanning the internal flames while ensuring they don't burn out. To prepare for this breathwork, practice the exhale. Take a short, sharp exhale out of your nose as if you were trying to blow out a candle. You will feel your belly pulling back as you exhale, helping force the air out. This is the exhale you will use for Breath of Fire.

Come to a comfortable seated position with your spine upright. Lift up through the crown of your head, relaxing your shoulders. Close your eyes. Inhale about two-thirds of your lung capacity, then take 20 short, sharp exhales as you previously practiced. Remember to focus on the exhale, allowing the inhale to happen naturally. With each one, feel your belly snapping back. It will feel like you are pumping your abdomen. After 20 exhales, take a deep inhale and hold the breath for a count of 10. Feel the air circulate throughout your torso, creating space and room for energy to roam. Take your normal exhale, letting all of the air out. This is one complete round. Practice a second round, ending with another long inhale and full exhale. Slowly open your eyes, observing the space you feel in your body and freedom in your energy.

Solar Plexus Visualization

Our energetic body is composed of seven chakras, or wheels of energy. The chakra system begins at the base of the pelvis and continues through the body to the crown of the head. The third chakra is the solar plexus, or Manipura chakra, and relates to the energy of Aries. This chakra sits at the bottom of the rib cage and relates to our willpower, how we assert ourselves, and our internal fire. When our third chakra is blocked, we feel disempowered. We are unable to make decisions and follow through with them, and we ultimately give our power away. We can also feel frustrated with ourselves, suffer from low self-esteem, and avoid taking action toward our soul's purpose. When balanced, though, this chakra helps us trust ourselves, empowers us to take action while not wavering in our decisions, and allows us to appreciate other people's strengths.

On the Aries Full Moon, work with the third chakra to bring it balance, strengthen it, and allow it to help align you with your soul's path. The following is a visualization meditation to help align and recharge your third chakra. If possible, try to do this meditation during the day of the Full Moon. You can also do it at night, but the day is best. Stand outside under the light of the Sun with your bare feet planted firmly on the Earth. Close your eyes and tilt your face toward the Sun, feeling its radiance shining down on you. Reach your arms toward the sky, as if to touch the Sun, and feel its light coming down through your arms toward your heart. Pause here for a moment, feeling each fingertip light up with the energy of the Sun. Slowly lower your hands to your solar plexus right below your rib cage, with your fingertips covering the space between your ribs. Take a deep inhale into this area, seeing it fill with yellow, golden light. Take 5 deep breaths like this, seeing an expanding ball of light at the base of your rib cage. Notice any tightness here and allow it to relax. Also, notice any feelings or visions that arise while breathing into this area. What is this area holding? Does it feel balanced? Does it feel free or restricted? What is it telling you about your willpower?

Release your hands down to your sides, but stay focused on the ball of yellow light at your solar plexus. Begin to see it slowly rotating clockwise. Continue to see the ball of light spinning for the next 5 breaths. When chakras are balanced and free of restriction, they spin evenly and smoothly. As you see your chakra turning, also visualize it radiating outward into the world. See it as your own personal Sun, shining your brilliance. Feel the Sun above you reflected in your solar plexus and feel your power to create the life of your soul's purpose. As you walk through the rest of your day, feel this area leading and empowering you.

CIRCLE SET UP

The Full Moon in Aries comes near the end of Libra Season. Both signs enjoy the company of others or time alone. You can choose to practice with friends this Full Moon or with just your own energy. Full Moons are generally beneficial times to gather with other like-minded people and share your experiences. It's a time when we can fully be seen and show up as we are, for others to accept us. If you practice in a group, make sure you are comfortable enough to speak freely about your feelings, your process of release, and your newly formed creations.

CIRCLE SET UP

Choose a quiet location to set up your Moon Circle, either inside or outside. Incorporate all the elements, especially the elements of Fire for Aries and Air for Libra. Have plenty of candles or an outside fire. You can incorporate air through auric sprays, feathers to fan the smudge sticks, and even wind chimes to hear the air moving around you. Also, represent Earth and Water to bring in all four elements. You can use crystals to represent the Earth. Carnelian, Fire Quartz, Aragonite, and Howlite are wonderful crystals to align with the energy of Aries. Tourmaline, Lapis Luzuli, Ametrine, Peach Moonstone, and Lepidolite are great crystals to align with Libra's energy. Bring in the Water element through a room diffuser, a vase with flowers in it, or just a simple metal bowl containing water. You can even set up your circle by an ocean, lake or river.

Gather all of your supplies and build your circle. Create an outline with your objects, anchoring the four directions—north, south, east, and west—with either a crystal or candle. If you are creating an altar, set it up in the westerly part of the circle, as this placement facilitates release. To set up an altar, line up crystals of your choice, flowers, and images that inspire you. Since this is a Fire Moon, create a place to burn what you are releasing. Have a metal dish or other container that can safely hold a burning paper. If you choose to burn paper inside, make sure your space is properly ventilated so the smoke has somewhere to go. It is recommended that most burning ceremonies take place outside for safety purposes, which may mean your entire circle takes place outside under the Full Moon.

As you set up the circle, create enough space for everyone to be comfortable. You can anchor the circle with a large crystal or crystal grid in the middle. Once the perimeter is set, cleanse the area with a dried herb bundle or space-clearing spray. Begin cleansing at the easterly point, moving to the south, west, north, then back to the east. Imagine a white light encompassing the circle, protecting it from any outside energies. Light your candles and cleanse yourself with the smudge stick or spray. If you are having guests join you, cleanse their energy before entering the circle. The best way to cleanse the energy is to start from the top of the head and move down to the bottom of the feet. Make sure to cleanse around the body, making a circle with the spray or stick. Do each arm and each leg, not forgetting the bottoms of the feet. Once everyone has entered the circle, pause for a moment to let the energy settle before you begin.

Follow your intuitive guidance when leading a circle. As a guide, begin with each member introducing themselves. Talk about the astrological energy of the day and how it is affecting each one of you. Share and learn from each other about your unique experiences with this Full Moon. Give plenty of space for each person to speak. Follow your conversation with the meditation practice to still the mind. You can then begin the rest of the practices in this book. Do them alone, but share as much, or as little, with the others as you like. Go over questions and continue to learn from each other's perspectives. You can also perform the burning ritual described after the practices. Then pull cards to gain insight and intuition from the Universe on how to move forward knowing that you have cleared away what you no longer want.

Close the circle by giving gratitude to everyone who chose to honor the Full Moon with you. Give thanks to the elements for supporting you and the energy of the Universe for guiding you along the way.

CARD READING

Reading Cards is a beautiful way to access your intuition and tap into your, and the Universe's, higher wisdom. Anyone can pull cards, as long as you are willing to receive the information they provide. You need no prior experience, or training, just an open and clear mind.

You may use any cards you like for this practice, including but not limited to: Tarot Cards, Animal Medicine Cards, Oracle Cards or any Affirmation Cards. You also can pull cards from a few decks to gain different perspectives. If you are new to card pulling, try to ask only one deck the same question, as asking different decks the same question can become quite confusing. Below are some general guidelines on how to pull cards. Please improvise as needed and above anything else, listen to your intuition.

Clear Your Mind
A settled, grounded mind is essential for pulling cards. The last thing you want is random thoughts running around when you are trying to receive clear answers from yourself. Practice the breath work and meditation in this workbook to prepare and settle your mind. You may also clear your mind using sound frequencies through singing bowls. These can either be crystal or metal bowls. Play the bowl, or bowls, for about 3-5 minutes to help rid your mind of external noise as you focus on the harmony of the sound.

CARD READING

Pick Your Deck

There are many different decks out there. You can choose as many as you like. Know, though, that they each provide you a different energy or medicine. Tarot Cards are the most popular and should be used carefully. Although very useful, Tarot cards can give the wrong impression if you interpret them harshly. Animal Medicine cards offer different types of messages from the animal realm which can help align with the spirit of nature. These cards give you the medicine you need to apply to your situation or question. Affirmation cards provide you with guidance in the form of words or phrases. When reading these cards, it is best to meditate on what the affirmation means for you. It is also helpful to repeat the affirmation a few times and see how it makes you feel. There are many other cards you can experiment with, like Goddess Cards, Angel Cards, and so on. The important thing to remember with any card is that they each have different angles and sides. There are often a few interpretations of the same card.

Shuffle

Shuffle the cards the easiest way for you. Some cards are smaller and can be shuffled like a regular deck of playing cards, while others with take some effort. If all else fails, spread them out on the floor in front of you then regather them. Keep a clear mind while shuffling. You can also repeat " I am open to receiving guidance and intuition." Refrain from asking your questions until the next step.

Aries Card Questions

You are free to ask the deck any questions you need answers to on this Full Moon. The following questions are meant to help you harness the energy of Aries through the cards to clarify some of these energies in your mind. This is a three-part card reading, where you'll ask the deck three questions. Before beginning, spread your freshly shuffled cards in a wide arc in front of you. Use your left middle finger to choose the card, first waving your hand slowly over the cards. You'll feel a magnetic pull, or slight tingle, in your fingertip when you hover over the right card. Chose one card at a time, taking a moment to breathe in between questions. Keep the cards flipped over until you pull all three.

What energy do I need to direct my internal fire?

What energy will help me align with my soul's purpose?

What energy will help me stay motivated on my path?

Take Them In

Once you have your cards, flip them over. Before looking up their meaning, sit with them for a moment and allow them to speak to you. Intuit your own meaning and interpretation of the card. What is the card trying to tell you? What are you trying to tell yourself? After a few moments with the cards, look up their meaning. Sit with that information, merging it with your intuitive meaning of the cards.

As with everything, enjoy this process. Do not worry if you are doing it right or wrong. Just follow your intuition, and trust the journey. Accept the cards you are dealt and use their energy wisely to help guide you when you need it the most.

BE SO COMMITTED TO
YOUR GROWTH
YOU ARE WILLING TO SAY
NO WITHOUT GUILT
AND YES WITHOUT FEAR.

———

SPIRIT DAUGHTER

ARIES PRACTICES

Under the Aries Full Moon, we have the opportunity to discover our purpose. It's a time to feel our soul and ask it want it wants. It's also a time to shed the lower vibrations of both Aries and Libra so we feel free to fulfill our life's mission while sharing it with other people. This Full Moon is full of excitement and passion, as it guides us to the reason we are alive. Feel the fire and intensity this Moon offers to burn through any block while aligning with your soul's path.

Over this Full Moon, commit to finding yourself. Aries gives you the energy and motivation needed to align with your life's mission. Notice if you are feeling any frustration and instead ask yourself what you can do with that energy. What steps can you take in finding your path and pursuing it? This Moon is very much about learning how to direct your energy. Aries asks that you do not act like a passive bystander in your life, but rather as an active participant. Take action this Full Moon in making your purpose a priority.

The practices of the Full Moon are designed to first help you find your purpose. It requires your commitment and willingness to open your mind. Your purpose may not be what you think it is, and it may not conform to your expectations. It may also take some experimentation to find it. This process can occur in one flash of insight, or it may take years to understand your life's mission. Finding your potential, though, is one of the most fulfilling things you can do. Many of us understand there is a reason our energy has chosen this body and this time to exist. We just don't know why. Be patient with the adventure of getting to know yourself as you explore various options.

When you do align with your purpose and feel you know how to spend your time, your world feels lighter. You know what to do and when to do it. It also informs your priorities and what choices you need to make to support them. Knowing your purpose also allows you to calmly explain your needs to your partners without the burden of having to justify your decisions. It gives you solid ground to stand on, and you understand the importance of your request. Knowing your purpose also makes it easier to know when things are non-negotiable with your partners. You know when to say yes. You also know when to say no without guilt.

The second part of these practices is designed to keep you motivated on your path once you've found it. It can be easy to burn out or lose your passion even if you're aligned with your purpose. Even the best dream loses its luster after years of living it. You have to tend to your internal fire to keep it going and remind yourself why it's important to keep showing up every day. This process can be challenging, as we often feel that once we find our purpose, the work is done. In fact, it is just beginning. You may not greet each day with the same enthusiasm, but it's important to celebrate your wins, cheer yourself on, and remind yourself why what you're doing is important. Your partners can help here too. Often we need another person's persecutive or even encouragement to keep us going when we've lost our passion. This is one of the reasons we share our lives with other people. They remind us where we've been and where we're going.

The following questions are designed to help you on the journey of this Full Moon. Really, what you are searching for is how you want to spend your time on this planet. This is an ongoing exploration and one that could take many Moons. Do not feel you have to answer all these questions or answer them all in one sitting. Take your time with them and allow the answers to unfold over time. Begin your exploration with these questions. But, more importantly, open your mind to the possibility of who you could be.

ARIES PRACTICES

1. Often times, finding our purpose requires letting go of who we think we should be. What past visions can you let go of? What visions belonging to other people should no longer affect you?

ARIES PRACTICES

2. What do you do when no one is watching? Or what would you do if you didn't have to explain it to your parents, friends, or other loved ones?

_____

_____

_____

_____

_____

_____

_____

_____

_____

_____

_____

_____

_____

_____

_____

_____

_____

_____

_____

_____

_____

_____

_____

_____

_____

ARIES PRACTICES

3. One clue to identifying your purpose is that you have energy when you are pursuing it. What activities give you energy and excite you?

ARIES PRACTICES

4. What activities do you get lost in to the point you forget about everything around you, even eating?

_____

_____

_____

_____

_____

_____

_____

_____

_____

_____

_____

_____

_____

_____

_____

_____

_____

_____

_____

_____

_____

_____

_____

_____

_____

_____

ARIES PRACTICES

5. What would your eight-year-old self be doing right now?

ARIES PRACTICES

6. Another clue to finding your purpose is to look at what makes you unique. Each of us is composed of a specific interaction of energies. We are each snowflakes with unique perceptions, history, and magic. What is your magic? What is something that makes you, you?

_____

_____

_____

_____

_____

_____

_____

_____

_____

_____

_____

_____

_____

_____

_____

_____

_____

_____

_____

_____

_____

_____

_____

_____

_____

_____

ARIES PRACTICES

7. Every dream has it challenges. Even your ideal life will have its off days. How you decide to spend your time will come with inherent problems that will often provide you the most growth. What types of challenges help you grow? Or what problems are you willing to face?

ARIES PRACTICES

8. Who are your biggest supporters and how can they help when you've lost your way? Remember to put yourself on this list.

_____

_____

_____

_____

_____

_____

_____

_____

_____

_____

_____

_____

_____

_____

_____

_____

_____

_____

_____

_____

_____

_____

_____

_____

_____

_____

_____

_____

ARIES PRACTICES

9. Finally, what is your legacy? What do you want to be remembered for doing?

ARIES PRACTICES

10. What are three things you can do this week to explore ways of finding your purpose? This can include finding a class, volunteering, or just spending time doing nothing.

LAST QUARTER: IN LEO

OCTOBER 28TH

Tonight we have the Last Quarter Moon, a time to fully release and create space before the Moon is new again. This Moon is positioned in the fierce, brave-hearted Leo, who always brings us to the heart of the matter. The pairing of the Moon, Leo, and the Sun in Scorpio can give us the courage to explore the deepest parts of ourselves and let go of what no longer serves our highest potential.

Leo brings us to our hearts, and the heart of the matter. This is a very direct energy, and it will bring issues of the heart right up to the surface. There is no guessing with a Leo Moon. If it's in your emotional body, it's going to be on the surface of your mind and your face. Leo, though, gives us the strength to face it all and never backs down from a challenge.

Scorpio's energy is fearless. She fearlessly calls in lessons to further her evolution. This energy wants us to go deep and explore our very consciousness. Coupled with a Leo Moon, Scorpio gives us the courage to explore the deepest parts of ourselves—the shadows and the buried skeletons. If we choose to, we can march right in there with the heart of Lion and shift those deepest parts into a higher vibration—one of trust, surrender, and faith. This is a powerful combination and can resolve the hardest issues we face.

This Moon is a powerful time to shed layers we've been living with for years out of familiarity and fear of the unknown. Know that in letting go of thoughts, feelings, and situations, we are telling the Universe that we are ready to receive something different. Ask yourself tonight, How can I face my deepest fears with love and compassion? How can I shift them into a higher vibration? Know the Moon is helping you on the continuous journey of your soul's evolution.

What are you willing to let go this
Last Quarter Moon to allow yourself to
receive new energy?

AFFIRMATIONS

Think of three people who can be role models of purpose for you. They can be someone in your life or someone you have never met. Name three qualities each of these people possess.

_____

_____

_____

_____

_____

_____

Now write three mantras based on these qualities that you can repeat to yourself every day.

Example: My friend Jackie works hard, confronts adversity, and trusts herself. Mantra: I trust myself to work hard and face adversity with grace.

_____

_____

_____

_____

_____

_____